The World's COOLEST Jobs

# STUNT PERFORMER

Alix Wood

**PowerKiDS**
press

New York

Published in 2014 by The Rosen Publishing Group, Inc.
29 East 21st Street, New York, NY 10010

Editor for Alix Wood Books: Eloise Macgregor
Designer: Alix Wood
US Editor: Joshua Shadowens
Researcher: Kevin Wood
Film Consultant: Christopher Drake

Library of Congress Cataloging-in-Publication Data

Wood, Alix.
 Stunt performer / by Alix Wood.
    pages cm. — (The World's Coolest Jobs)
 Includes index.
 ISBN 978-1-4777-5999-8 (library binding) — ISBN 978-1-4777-6000-0 (pbk.) —
ISBN 978-1-4777-6002-4 (6-pack)
 1. Stunt performers—Juvenile literature. I. Title.
 PN1995.9.S7W66 2014
 791.4302'8—dc23

                      2013020351

Manufactured in the United States of America

CPSIA Compliance Information: Batch #W14PK2: For Further Information contact Rosen Publishing, New York, New York at 1-800-237-9932

# Contents

# What Is a Stunt Performer?

A stuntman or stuntwoman performs stunts for use in movies or television. **Daredevils** perform stunts for entertainment or for the thrill, such as escape artists, motorcycle display teams, or tightrope walkers.

A stunt performer is a specialized actor trained to perform dangerous stunts. He or she may take the place of regular actors in a film or television production when stunts are required. Stunt performers are used in fight scenes and other dangerous situations on set. Stunt coordinators are trained stunt performers who **choreograph** stunts.

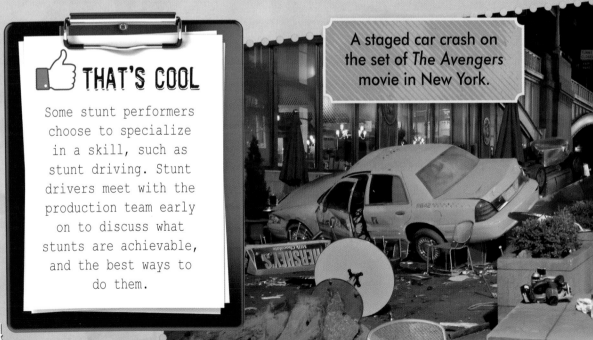

👍 THAT'S COOL

Some stunt performers choose to specialize in a skill, such as stunt driving. Stunt drivers meet with the production team early on to discuss what stunts are achievable, and the best ways to do them.

A staged car crash on the set of *The Avengers* movie in New York.

Daredevil feats were popular
in the 1800s. Between 1859
and 1896 there were many
wire-walking attempts across
Niagara Gorge, a large gorge
and waterfall on the border
between Canada and the US.
In 1876 23-year-old Italian
Maria Spelterini was the first
woman to cross Niagara Gorge
on a tightrope. She made four
separate crossings over 18
days. One time she crossed
wearing peach baskets strapped
to her feet! On another
crossing she was blind-folded,
and on another had her ankles
and wrists chained!

Maria Spelterini crossing
Niagara Gorge on a tightrope
with peach baskets on her feet!

Even though stunt performers
take safety precautions, their work
is still very dangerous. Because of
this, stunt performers tend to be
well-paid for their work. Stunts seen in film
and television include car crashes, high falls, and
explosions. In movies safety equipment can be used
and then **edited out** afterward. Performing stunts
in front of a live audience is more risky as the safety
equipment can't be used. Performers usually belong
to professional organizations which help them if they
get injured in an accident.

# Learning the Ropes

To become a stunt performer, some people go to special schools where professionals teach them how to do stunts. Most people do not go to a stunt school, though. They learn the skills from other more experienced stuntmen.

In many countries, stunt people need to join a union to work on movie or television show productions. To become a member of a union they usually need to have done some work as an **extra** on television or in a movie. Working as an extra is a good way to become familiar with film sets and perhaps get to see stunt work in action.

After doing some work as an extra, it may be possible to register as a stunt performer and start doing minor stunts like punches. Useful skills to develop include learning **stage combat**, rock climbing, skiing, sky diving, scuba diving, and martial arts. Experience in high-performance driving, horseback riding, and firearm use can be useful too.

Brad Pitt talks to some extras on the set of *In The Land Of Blood And Honey*.

## 👍 THAT'S COOL

The first stuntmen were comedians like the Keystone Kops and Buster Keaton. They learned through trial and error! If they needed a scene where a man hung from a steel girder hundreds of feet (m) above the ground, they didn't make a fake steel girder above a padded mat, they found an actor willing to hang from an actual steel girder.

Silent movie star Harold Lloyd hanging from the hands of a clock high above the street in *Safety Last!* Lloyd did many of these dangerous stunts himself.

## FACT FILE

**Skills a stunt performer needs to learn**

**Tumbling** – to roll and fall safely using somersaults, handsprings, shoulder rolls, break falls, and dive rolls

**Using an air ram** – to safely use hydraulics and compressed air which catapult a performer into the air

**High Falls** – to safely perform a variety of falls from three stories or higher, landing on an air bag or cardboard boxes

**Swordplay** – to perform choreographed swordfights

**Horsework** – to ride horses while performing stunts such as falling off or jumping onto a horse, or swordfighting

**Wirework** – to use rigs, harnesses, and vests to perform aerial stunts, such as flying or falling action sequences

# Stunt Doubles

A stunt double is a stunt person who acts as a skilled replacement for an actor or actress during any dangerous sequences in movies and television.

Many stunt performers work as **body doubles**. They are chosen because they look similar to the actor they are standing in for. Stunt doubles may often be kept on-set at all times in case they are needed. Many stunt doubles have long careers as part of a star actor's support crew, along with the star's cooks, trainers, dressers, and assistants. Stunt doubles for Eddie Murphy, John Wayne, Harrison Ford, Steve Martin, Salman Khan, and Michael Landon have been associated with their lead actors for decades.

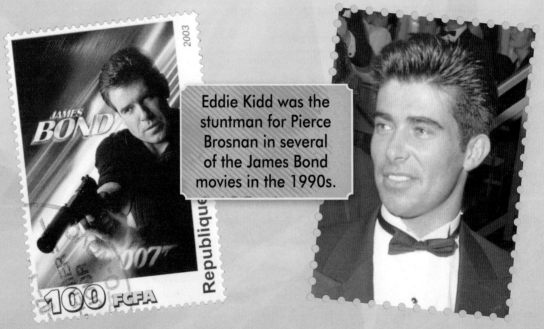

Eddie Kidd was the stuntman for Pierce Brosnan in several of the James Bond movies in the 1990s.

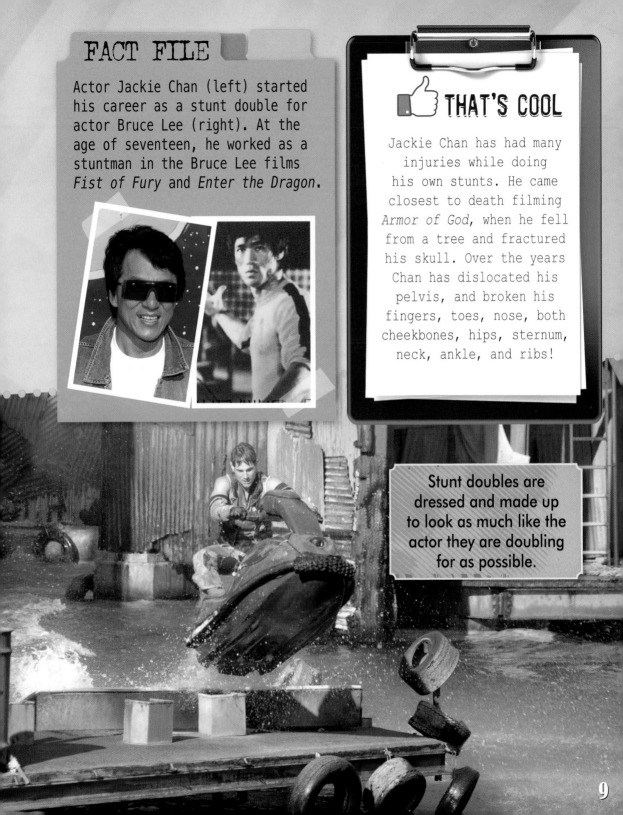

# FACT FILE

Actor Jackie Chan (left) started his career as a stunt double for actor Bruce Lee (right). At the age of seventeen, he worked as a stuntman in the Bruce Lee films *Fist of Fury* and *Enter the Dragon*.

## 👍 THAT'S COOL

Jackie Chan has had many injuries while doing his own stunts. He came closest to death filming *Armor of God*, when he fell from a tree and fractured his skull. Over the years Chan has dislocated his pelvis, and broken his fingers, toes, nose, both cheekbones, hips, sternum, neck, ankle, and ribs!

Stunt doubles are dressed and made up to look as much like the actor they are doubling for as possible.

# Stunt Driving Skills

Stunt driving is a high-adrenaline cool job. Stunt drivers can earn a living in several ways, in car commercials, in film and tv, or performing live stunts for entertainment.

Almost every action movie features some type of car stunt work. Whether it is a big car chase or a single car sliding to a stop on a specific **mark**, these maneuvers are all done by highly trained stunt performers. The stunts are planned, choreographed, rehearsed, and performed with precision. Timing can be critical and if one driver is a little off their mark or just a few seconds too late or early, the stunt can be ruined, or someone could get hurt.

Stunt drivers use a ramp to make the car start driving on two wheels. Then they drive using minute changes to the **throttle** and the steering. The tires need a little extra air in them, but other than that the car needs no modification.

To safely film a car explosion all the windows are usually removed from the car. That includes the glass in the side mirrors, the windshield and the back window. If the illusion of glass is needed, specially produced sugar glass is used. As much as possible of the car's interior is removed, too. If the remaining bits of car interior are **flammable**, they are soaked in water.

## 👍 THAT'S COOL

To make a car flip over, an explosive charge is set near the rear wheel opposite the driver's side. The driver usually sets off the explosives himself using a switch. The driver turns the wheel towards the side where the explosives are at the same time as the explosion goes off. The force of this flips the car.

# Playing with Fire

Any film scene where fire is involved is always going to be dangerous. Scenes where someone is actually set on fire are among the most dangerous ever filmed.

When a stunt person gets set on fire they need to wear layers of protective clothing made of fire-resistant materials like **asbestos**. First, thick layers of protective cream are smeared all over the stunt actor's skin. The actor puts on several layers of long underwear and a protective face mask all soaked in protective gel. Usually the head and hands are covered with a special hood and gloves, too. The hood is quite large and the movie will often need editing to make sure it can't be seen on film. Inside the hood there is a breathing tube connected to a small oxygen tank.

The actor puts normal clothes on top, which are set on fire using a special gel. A paramedic and a team with fire extinguishers get ready in case they are needed.

The fire team must put out the flames in under two minutes or the stunt person may burn and breathe in lethal heat and smoke.

Cars used in stunt scenes aren't straight out of the showroom. They're modified with added safety equipment like roll cages and fire extinguishers, mountings for cameras and any gear needed to accomplish the stunt itself.

If a stuntman doesn't wear a hood he needs to trust his team will put out the flames in time.

People who work with explosive devices are called **pyrotechnicians**. They work closely with stunt artists to stage explosions and fires that look as real and exciting as possible, while still being safe. To create a car crash and big explosion but keep the driver safe, pyrotechnicians sometimes fill every space in the car with insulating foam and fit fire extinguishers which can be activated by a switch on the dashboard.

## 👍 THAT'S COOL

In 2004, US stuntman Ted Batchelor set the record for the longest full-body burn, at 2 minutes, 38 seconds. Doesn't sound too long? Try counting to 158 and imagine being on fire the whole time!

# Stage Fighting Skills

Stunt performers need to learn how to create convincing fight scenes without causing harm to themselves or other performers. This fighting is called stage combat.

Stage combat choreography is usually learned step by step, and practiced very slowly at first. Then the actors will increase to a speed that is convincing but also safe for the performers. Even stage combat is risky, and it is preferable for actors to have as much training and experience as possible.

Stage combat includes slaps, punches, kicks, throws, and holds, as well as armed fighting, with swords or even fantasy weapons like lightsabers.

 **THAT'S COOL**

Stage actors involved in fight scenes have a "fight call" before each performance. This is a brief rehearsal so that the actors can practice the fight and increase their **muscle memory**. Muscle memory is a phenomenon that happens when you repeat an action. Your body remembers the moves and they become second nature.

## Selling a Punch

If the camera is positioned at the right angle, a movie punch can miss by quite a distance and still look realistic. The actors need to use a technique called "selling" the punch.

1) The person throwing the punch should look angry, punch convincingly, and look satisfied after the blow.

2) For the actor taking the punch, timing is critical. He or she will use techniques such as head movements, keeping the lips loose, and letting the body go limp for a second after the punch to make it appear to have hit its target.

2) Film editors then cut the scene to make it even more dramatic and convincing. The sound effects they add all help add to the realism.

## FACT FILE

When someone is being strangled in a stage fight, the actors make it look as though the attacker is in control. In reality, it is the person acting as the victim that controls the action. The attacker places his hands around the other actor's neck, with the other actors hands on top. Instead of trying to strangle the victim, he or she will try with all their strength to remove their hands, while the victim fights to hold them in place. The victim therefore always has control of any pressure around their neck and the struggle looks very realistic.

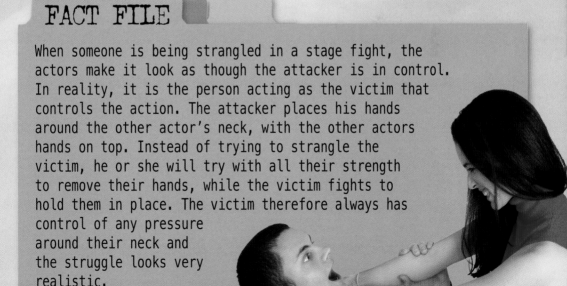

# Fight Choreography

Stunt performers need to know how to fight convincingly and safely using various weapons. The fight coordinator is responsible for organizing fight scenes.

A fight coordinator's relationship with the stunt team is like a film director's with the actors. He or she must plan and oversee the fight scenes while also having an understanding of the whole movie and the scenes' relationship within it. The fights need to be suitable for the film and its audience. If it is a young children's film, for example, it mustn't be too violent.

## FACT FILE

Bob Anderson was a famous fight choreographer with a long movie career. He worked on the first *Star Wars* trilogy, the *Lord of the Rings* trilogy, and the *Pirates of the Caribbean* movies. An ex-Royal Marine, he had competed in **fencing** at the 1952 Olympics. He acted the fight scenes for the character Darth Vader in the *Star Wars* films, too.

Steven McMichael was the fight coordinator on *The Hobbit* trilogy. He made sure the hundreds of actors, stuntmen, and doubles making up the cast were trained. He thought up and directed the fight scenes, devised weapon training and workouts for everyone from A-list stars to untrained extras.

*The Hobbit* was filmed in 3D. Because the 3D camera picks up depth, the stunt actors couldn't miss when they fought as 2D actors can. They had to actually make contact. To get around this, the actors would use foam sticks wrapped with green screen tape. The actors could safely make contact during filming and the weapons were then drawn in digitally afterwards.

## 👍 THAT'S COOL

Steven McMichael's official credit on *The Hobbit* trilogy was "sword master," which is the New Zealand film industry's name for a fight choreographer.

Filming in front of a green screen or using green tape means the green can be selected and deleted using special software. A new background or weapon can be put in its place. Weather broadcasts often use this technology to put different maps behind the presenter.

# Riding Horses and Bikes

Stunts on horseback, or on bikes and motorbikes require special skills. First stunt performers need to be very capable on a bike or horse, and then take it to the next level.

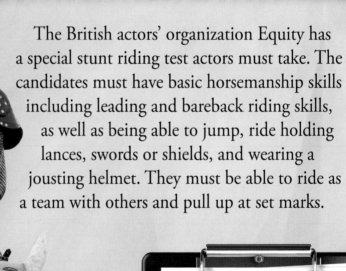

The British actors' organization Equity has a special stunt riding test actors must take. The candidates must have basic horsemanship skills including leading and bareback riding skills, as well as being able to jump, ride holding lances, swords or shields, and wearing a jousting helmet. They must be able to ride as a team with others and pull up at set marks.

This stunt performer is Roman riding, with one foot on each horse. He must trust his horses!

 **THAT'S COOL**

Horse riding stunts often include being dragged along behind a horse by the stirrup. The horse has to be specially trained too, so it doesn't spook when dragging the actor.

To perform motorbike stunts it's important to wear the right equipment, such as protective clothing and a helmet.

## FACT FILE

Knievel promoted wearing helmets for bike safety.

Evel Knievel was a motorcycle daredevil. His televised stunts are among the most watched sporting events of all time. Robert Craig Knievel started his career as a motocross rider. In need of money he started performing stunts on his motorcycle. His first jump was over a box of rattlesnakes and two mountain lions. Soon, Knievel was regularly jumping over rows of cars and trucks. His most famous stunt was in 1974, when he attempted to jump the Snake River Canyon in Idaho, on a rocket-propelled motorcycle. A malfunction caused the bike's parachute to open early and ruin the jump.

# Falling With Style!

Learning how to fall safely from high places is essential. A stunt performer will usually have either top class gymnastics skills or be an expert rock climber. Agility is essential for the job.

Basic falls and falls from heights is standard work for the stunt professional. They need to be able to safely fall from three stories or higher. They'll often have to perform a variety of falls, such as back falls, twisting falls, or "bull dogging" (flying through the air and coming down on another stunt performer). Stunt performers use mini trampolines or air rams to propel themselves higher in the air.

The Russian swing is a swing platform between two A-frames which can throw a performer even farther than an air ram can. An experienced Russian swing performer can fly over a house!

## THAT'S COOL

As stunt performers say, "it isn't the fall that hurts but the stopping!" In the early days, high falls were done onto hay. This was replaced by a more high-tech solution, empty cardboard boxes! When carefully stacked they collapse which breaks the fall. Airbags are used now too, but in spaces they don't fit, it's cardboard boxes!

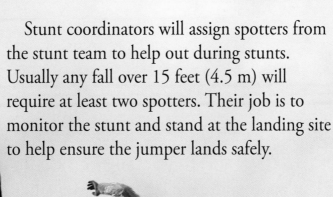

Stunt coordinators will assign spotters from the stunt team to help out during stunts. Usually any fall over 15 feet (4.5 m) will require at least two spotters. Their job is to monitor the stunt and stand at the landing site to help ensure the jumper lands safely.

## FACT FILE

Knowing what your body is doing and controlling it in the air is called "air sense." Not everyone has it. This sense will make you valuable in the stunt business. A stunt performer with air sense at an audition could jump off a mini trampoline, dive over a desk, and reach out and grab a laptop as they sail over the table. Having air sense would get them the job over the ones who just cleared the table.

# Underwater Stunts

Underwater stunts have unique demands. Stunt performers need to be able to hold their breath for long periods and be happy underwater in stressful situations.

Many underwater stunts involve the stunt performer acting out the act of drowning, often fully clothed and in full make up and wigs! Sometimes the movie will need actors fighting underwater. It is very tiring acting underwater. Breathing tubes can be hidden in clothing so the actor can breathe during long takes. Moving in and out of the water can affect a diver's ears, so often the stunt performers will stay underwater until the filming sequence is finished.

David Blaine, the American illusionist and endurance artist, submerged himself in a water-filled sphere in Lincoln Center in New York City. He was in the sphere for seven days and nights, using tubes for air and food.

# FACT FILE

Harry Houdini, born Erik Weisz, was an **escapologist**. He was responsible for pioneering many stunts that are still performed today. Houdini performed several underwater escapes. He was handcuffed and sealed inside a large milk can filled with water, and would invite members of the audience to see if they could hold their breath along with him. Houdini was once locked in a sealed casket underwater in a hotel swimming pool for an hour and a half. In his most famous stunt, the Chinese Water Torture Cell, he was suspended upside-down in a locked glass and steel cabinet full of water. The act meant that Houdini had to hold his breath for more than three minutes!

A sightseeing boat at the base of Niagara Falls

## 👍 THAT'S COOL

In 1901 63-year-old schoolteacher Annie Edson Taylor was the first person to successfully go over Niagara Falls. She went over inside a wooden barrel. She used a specially designed barrel filled with padding. Amazingly, she survived the 173-foot (53 m) plunge with little more than a small gash on her head.

# Stunts in the Air

Since the 1920s, Hollywood filmmakers have used flight stunts in movies. Stunt pilots have to have exceptional flying skills and attention to detail to be successful and survive.

In recent films there have been some spectacular stunts in the air. For the 2012 movie *The Dark Knight Rises*, the opening sequence involved four stuntmen lowering themselves on cables out of the cargo doors of a Hercules plane onto a smaller plane. In some shots this smaller plane is replaced by a glider. The stuntmen climb onto the glider, get the villain out of the plane, which then explodes and crashes to the ground.

Movies can require World War I and II aircraft dogfights, helicopter tricks, or jet fighters spinning out of control. Stunt pilot Corkey Fornof thinks flying stunts is a matter of mind control. He describes approaching the hangar he had to fly through during filming of a James Bond movie with his brain yelling "don't do it!" But he still did!

Barnstorming was popular in the 1920s, where stunt pilots would perform tricks with airplanes. **Wing walking** and transferring from a plane to another plane or car were popular stunts. Stunt flyer Paul Mantz specialized in flying through buildings. In 1932, he flew a plane through an aircraft hangar for the film *Air Mail*. The most elaborate trick he performed was flying an airplane through a billboard.

## FACT FILE

Back in the early years of flight, Ethel Dare, born Margie Hobbs, was a pioneer wing walker. She walked along the wings of speeding **biplanes**, and was the first woman to hop to another plane during the stunt. She would stand on the edge of the wing and fall off backwards with a rope clenched in her teeth to stop her fall. With the special mouthpiece clenched between her teeth, she would twirl around behind the plane's propeller!

In this stunt a wing walker lifts himself into a passing helicopter!

# Stunts on a Wire

Knowing how to tie a good knot could be the most important skill a stunt performer has. When you are hanging off a helicopter at 400 feet (122 m), you want to be sure of the knot that is holding you.

Many of the movies produced today use stunt rigging. Rigging is the wires, pulleys, and other gear that stunt people use to help them perform controlled midair stunts. Knowing how to rig these kinds of stunts is as much a science as it is an art. Riggers need to understand loads and work out the strength of the cable they use.

## 👍 THAT'S COOL

A wire rigger uses special harnesses, rails, wires, and pulleys which can make an actor appear to fly. Many feature films such as *Harry Potter* and *Superman* use this technique to make actors appear to fly through the air.

Swinging high in the air while trying to act like a superhero isn't easy. The wires are edited out of the film afterwards.

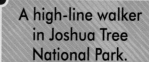

## FACT FILE

Frenchman Charles Blondin was a famous tightrope walker who crossed the Niagara Falls gorge, getting more and more theatrical with every crossing. He crossed the span on foot, on stilts, blindfolded, in a sack, carrying a man on his back, and even pushing a wheelbarrow across ahead of him. In the most bizarre crossing of all, Blondin stopped halfway across the falls, sat down on the tightrope, and cooked and ate an omelet!

Charles Blondin carrying his manager on his back

# Still Want To Be a Stunt Performer?

If you are interested in a career as a stunt performer, start to learn some of the skills you may need. Take up a martial art, rock climbing, or scuba diving. Learn to ride a horse and try to get fit.

Stunt work is a cool job, but it does have some bad points. Performers can be hurt or even killed. Stunt work is also not steady work, and actors usually only work on a movie-by-movie basis, often only for a single stunt that is filmed over just a day or two. If they are lucky they can double for the lead actor and work for a few months. Stuntmen also have to travel to get work. Being away from home a lot can mean you get homesick.

Departures

| DESTINATION | BOARDING TIME | GATE | STATUS |
| --- | --- | --- | --- |
| DUBAI | 17:35 | 15 | FINAL CALL |
| SYDNEY | 17:50 | 04 | BOARDING |
| MELBOURNE | 18:05 | 16 | BOARDING IN 5 MINS |
| BUENOS AIRES | 18:10 | 02 | BOARDING IN 5 MINS |
| RAROTONGA | 18:25 | 07 | BOARDING IN 10 MINS |
| LOS ANGELES | 18:35 | 01 | BOARDING IN 25 MINS |
| SAN FRANCISCO | 18:35 | 06 | BOARDING IN 35 MINS |
| LOS ANGELES | 18:50 | | BOARDING IN 35 MINS |
| RAROTONGA | 20:10 | | BOARDING IN 50 MINS |
| LONDON | 21:05 | | PLEASE WAIT |
| SYDNEY | 22:05 | | |

18:00

Getting to travel around the world can be a good point too, though!

28

A lot of people think that stunt performers must be big risk takers. This is not true. A stunt performer never just climbs on a roof and jumps into a swimming pool. He or she would check the distance first, see how deep the pool is, and make a calculation as to how far to jump. The whole point is to make it to the next day, to make this stunt work, and the next one, and the next one. Getting hurt means not making money. Stunt people also count on the rest of the stunt team around them to be level-headed.

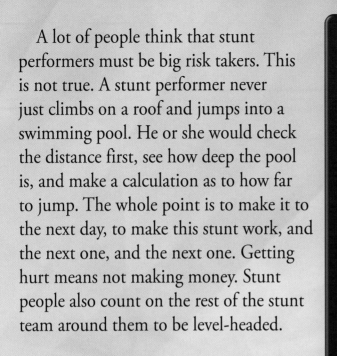

## 👍 THAT'S COOL

Stunt performers need to be tough. Not just physically tough but also able to take rejection. Inner strength and commitment are important to get through the hard times. Also they need to be polite and hard working, and not annoy anyone on set. Reputations stick, and it is a small industry.

# Glossary

**asbestos** (as-BES-tus)
A grayish mineral used to make materials that are fireproof.

**biplanes** (BY-playnz)
A biplane is a fixed-wing aircraft with two main wings.

**body doubles**
(BAH-dee DUH-bulz)
Movie actors who substitute for leading performers, especially in distance shots or scenes not involving the face.

**choreograph**
(KOR-ee-uh-graf)
To plan the sequence of steps and movements for a dance or fight scene in a movie.

**daredevils** (DER-deh-vulz)
Recklessly bold people.

**edited out**
(EH-dit-ed OWT)
Removed from a film by cutting or digitally editing.

**escapologist**
(us-kayp-AH-luh-jist)
An entertainer who specializes in freeing himself or herself from confinement.

**extra** (EK-stra)
A person hired to play a minor part, as in a crowd scene in a movie or on television.

**fencing** (FEN-sing)
The art or practice of attack and defense with a sword.

**flammable** (FLA-muh-bul)
Capable of being easily set on fire and of burning rapidly.

**mark** (MARK)
A mark on the floor, usually an X or T made with tape, used in the film industry to show actors where to stand.

**muscle memory**
(MUH-sul MEM-oh-ree)
A type of movement that muscles gradually become familiar with.

**pyrotechnicians**
(py-roh-tek-NIH-shunz)
People responsible for handling and using fireworks and other explosive devices.

**stage combat**
(STAYJ KOM-bat)
To create the illusion of physical combat without harming the performers.

**throttle** (THRAH-tul)
A handle or pedal that controls the supply of fuel to an engine.

**wing walking**
(WING WAHK-ing)
The act of moving on the wings of an airplane during flight.

## WEBSITES

Due to the changing nature of Internet links, PowerKids Press has developed an online list of websites related to the subject of this book. This site is updated regularly. Please use this link to access the list:

**www.powerkidslinks.com/wcj/stunt**

# Read More

Gonzalez, Lissette. *Stunt Performers and Stunt Doubles.* Dangerous Jobs. New York: PowerKids Press, 2007.

O'Shei, Tim. *The World's Most Dangerous Stunts.* The World's Top Tens. Mankato, MN: Capstone Press, 2006.

Regan, Lisa. *Movie Star.* Stage School. New York: Windmill Books, 2012.

# Index